Endorsements

"Life is short and before we know it, it has passed us by. Don't let it pass you by. This book provides insight on how network marketing can help you achieve your goals and dreams!"

- Vince Poscente
CEO of the Goal Acceleration Institute,
NY Times Bestselling Author and Olympian

"This book is the reality check you can take to the bank and cash. You will discover a new and powerful way to build a successful home-based business. If time and money freedom is something you desire, read every word of this extraordinary book now."

- Peggy McColl
NY Times Bestselling Author & Online Marketing Expert

"This book simplifies what you need to do (due diligence) regarding selecting a network marketing business. A must read!"

- Garrett McGrath
President, The Association of Network Marketing Professionals

"Deborah MacDonald is one of the smartest and highest integrity leaders I have ever met in the network marketing industry. She is smart enough to know how to strategically invest her residual income into real estate in a way that allows that money to compound and grow exponentially. I highly recommend you follow what she teaches. She is the real deal."

- Lisa Larter
Master Strategist, Business Coach, Speaker, Author

"Get your copy today to gain an understanding how Network Marketing can allow you to "create freedom" and "live a life you and your family will love!" This is a great book for those looking at Network Marketing for the first time."

- Cathy and Bernie Dohmann
Ambassadors, Evolv Health

"Deborah is an impressive network marketing professional, real estate investor and business coach in the Ottawa area who I have personally known for over 3 years. Her educational book is another great tool to help anyone build a successful residual income business."

- Rich Danby
President, Rich Ottawa Investments Inc.

CREATING FREEDOM

What you *need* to know to be successful in network marketing

by

Deborah MacDonald

Copyright © 2014 (Deborah MacDonald)

All rights reserved worldwide

No part of this publication may be reproduced in any form, by photostat, microfilm, xerography, digitally, or any other means, which are now known or to be invented or incorporated into any information retrieval system, electronic or mechanical, either whole or in part, without the express written permission of the rightful copyright owner.

Violations of this copyright notice will be enforced to the fullest extent of the law.

Dedication

This book, *Creating Freedom*, is dedicated to everyone who is seeking freedom, more time, increased income and a better lifestyle. It is for those who want to have a rewarding business and meaningful life based on residual/royalty type income through network marketing, instead of just trading time for money. And, it is definitely for those who want to pursue their dreams and never give up!

Although I have spent the last 13 years in the network marketing profession, I came into it with skepticism and a closed corporate mindset. After learning how lucrative and rewarding this model can be, I made a decision to study it and put it into practice, just like I did with my previous careers. My main problem was I did not fully understand it, and the majority of people I meet do not comprehend it either. This is why I wrote the book - to share my own due diligence process for evaluating a network marketing business, with the overall aim to elevate the profession itself.

If you're tired of living paycheck to paycheck and want more out of life, then this book is for you. If you are ready to truly pursue your goals and live a dream lifestyle, then this book is definitely for you.

Acknowledgements

First and foremost, I would like to thank my family – my husband, Jeff for his love and valuable support for the past 30 years and who already has another book in mind for me. To my amazing children, Stacey and Kevin, I am so grateful for their incredible wisdom, and their unwavering support - I love them so very much. And, finally to my Mom, who at 89 still asks me how my business is going. She is the most amazing parent and the guiding light in my life.

I would also like to thank my sister, Joanne, who introduced me to the industry. If it wasn't for her, I would not be writing this book. She encouraged me to look at this as a profession and to learn from the successful leaders who have already earned millions in the industry. She believed in me and for that I will always be grateful. Unfortunately her life was cut short and she passed away from breast cancer at the age of 53. She is, and always will be, my spiritual guide. I'm so blessed to have had the love of a sister who was my best friend and mentor and brought me such incredible encouragement.

To my sponsors in my primary company, Cathy and Bernie Dohmann, I am truly privileged to receive amazing coaching, mentoring and support, from them on a daily basis. They are one of the most inspirational, dynamic and successful leadership teams in the industry. They know how to make this business fun.

To my friend, Lisa Larter, thank you for being such a dynamic strategist and great business coach. When I tell Lisa my plans to do something, she is the catalyst that ignites the spark in me to get it off the ground.

I would also like to acknowledge my good friend and New York Times Best Selling Author, Peggy McColl for her practical advice and sound encouragement. Thank you, Peggy for being a tremendous inspiration and role model for me.

I want to recognize Vince Poscente, world renowned Olympian and New York Times Best Selling Author for his stirring motivation, his 'cut to the chase' encouragement and his 'seal team' style mentorship. Vince, you have significantly impacted my life.

I would also like to thank Garrett McGrath, President, Association of Network Marketing Professionals, for his incredible guidance and his astonishing wisdom regarding this industry. I'm so very blessed to be in his company.

I want to thank all my remarkable clients and fans who continue to buy my products, read my blog posts and share my content. I am forever grateful.

Finally, I would like to thank all of my team members from coast to coast, for embracing the network marketing business model and for being part of my team. Without you, my life would not be fulfilled. You truly are change-makers.

Contents

WHY I WROTE THIS BOOK 1

PART ONE: *IS NETWORK MARKETING FOR YOU?* 3

Chapter One What is your why? 5
   Is it financial freedom? 6
   Is it about having more time? 6

Chapter Two Why this business model is for you 8

Chapter Three What should you look for in a network marketing company? .. 13

Chapter Four The difference between traditional business and a network marketing business 17

Chapter Five Understand the power of leverage 21

Chapter Six Evaluate the industry trends 23

PART TWO: *MISCONCEPTIONS OF NETWORK MARKETING* 27

Chapter Seven Do people at the top make all the money? 29

Chapter Eight Do you have to involve family and friends? 33

Chapter Nine Do you need business or sales skills to be successful? 37

Chapter Ten What if you don't like to sell? 41

Chapter Eleven Can you buy your way to the top? 45

Chapter Twelve Can you really make money in network marketing? 49

PART THREE: *THE REALITY OF NETWORK MARKETING* . 53

Chapter Thirteen What are the pros and cons? 55
    Pros 56
    Cons 59

Chapter Fourteen Home business tax benefits 61

Chapter Fifteen Understand you're not alone 65

Chapter Sixteen How much do you have to invest? 69

Chapter Seventeen How to avoid high pressure sales tactics 73

Chapter Eighteen How much money and time is required? 77

Chapter Nineteen How the compensation plan works 81
    Unilevel Compensation Plan 82
    Stair Step Breakaway Compensation Plan 83
    Forced Matrix Compensation Plan 84
    Binary Compensation Plan 85
    Hybrid Compensation Plan 86

Chapter Twenty How to fast track your network marketing success 87
    Step 1: Use Your Own Products 88
    Step 2: Stop Selling and Recommend 88
    Step 3: Treat It Like a Real Business 89
    Step 4: Find a Coach to Mentor You 89
    Step 5: Invite People to Join Your Team 90
    Step 6: Mentor Your Team 90
    Step 7: Create Residual Income 91

CALL TO ACTION: *IF YOU'RE SERIOUS ABOUT CREATING FREEDOM THROUGH NETWORK MARKETING* 93

ABOUT THE AUTHOR 95

BONUS GIFT 97

Why I Wrote This Book

This book will transform the way you think about the network marketing profession.

Are you one of the millions of individuals working sixty hours a week, living pay check to pay check, struggling just to keep your head above water? Then all of sudden, something goes wrong in your life and you realize you don't have enough money to pay for it, or time to generate any additional income to help solve the problem? Are you feeling exhausted, overwhelmed, or stressed out, to the point that you don't even have time to think about financial freedom or a dream lifestyle, much less make it happen?

It doesn't have to be that way. There is another option if you're ready to let go of the struggle. My book, *Creating Freedom* will give you a full understanding of what you need to know about the network marketing business model and how it can change your finances, your life and your future.

Over the years, I have become very passionate about the network marketing profession. I understand the power of leverage and the power of building a network for cash flow and wealth creation through residual income.

Most people join a network marketing company based on emotion, rather than on facts and due diligence. You see, when I invest thousands and thousands of dollars into an income property, I make sure to do my due diligence - the analysis of the facts and the numbers, so that I am confident with my decision. This is the reason why I have written this book.

This book is not about the 'how-to'. It's about everything you need to know, to feel confident about choosing this leveraged based income model and how to select the right company to partner with. It's the due diligence process you need to do before you jump in.

Years ago, I realized that I wanted a different lifestyle for both my family and myself, and that's when network marketing came knocking on my door. It was at a time in my life when there had been a family tragedy. I knew I needed to make radical changes to help me get through the grief.

My husband, an air force pilot, and myself, a corporate training executive, were each working 60-80 hours a week. At the same time, we were raising children, moving to new cities and even countries, every couple of years. I felt like we were on a treadmill, never slowing down to enjoy the fruits of our labour.

It was then that I made a decision to put this network marketing business model into effect, after following a thorough evaluation and due diligence assessment. That's when I discovered the real secret to freedom - leveraging both time and money!

Over the next ten years, I became a successful network marketing professional, real estate investor and mentor to successful business owners and entrepreneurs. My success has been a result of taking my network marketing business profits and using them to make smart real estate investments. I started doing this in 2004 when I was just like you – and wanted something different. You see, I am a big believer in building assets.

Today I own many real estate income properties (these are buildings other people pay me to live in) and I choose the hours I want to work. I have a large network marketing team and travel all over North America to events to support them. And my real estate investment portfolio has grown from zero to over three million dollars in a very short period of time.

So, what qualifies me to help you? I did not win the lottery. I did not work 100 hours a week to do this. I did not bury myself in debt. I simply chose to create freedom and live my dream. And now I invite you to live yours!

Here's to living your dream life!

Deborah MacDonald
Entrepreneur | Investor | Author

www.deborahmacdonald.com

Part One:

Is Network Marketing for You?

Chapter One

What is your why?

Before you jump into any business opportunity at all, sit down and really think about why you want it. Why do you want to go into business at all? Why do you want to get into network marketing? Why are you reading this book for more information?

Your 'why' will be unique to you, but it's important you understand exactly what's driving you to search for something different.

> *"All our dreams can come true if we have the courage to pursue them."*
>
> *– Walt Disney*

Is it financial freedom?

At this point, most people will immediately think their 'why' is earning an extra income. Some will think they're looking for a way to replace the income they earn from a job. Others will aim more towards building up a profitable business in order to achieve financial freedom. And some will look at this as a means to create a legacy income to pass on to their children.
Aiming at the money aspect is completely logical. The idea of being able to create a sustainable, profitable business is very common with a large percentage of the population.

However, aiming at the money is a 'what' – it's not your 'why'.

You see, if your goal is to earn extra income or replace your salary or create financial freedom, you're focused on what you can achieve, but you're not taking into account WHY you want it. You need to look a little deeper and work out exactly WHY you want the additional money in the first place.

What will having extra income or replacing your salary or achieving financial freedom achieve for you and your family?

Is it about having more time?

Really think about what you're trying to accomplish. The big picture for many people is earning enough money to allow them to take more time off to spend with family and friends. Some people love the idea of being able to earn money at home so they have more time to spend with the kids while they're growing up.

For some people, it's about having enough money to travel more and experience what the world has to offer. For others, it's about having the financial freedom to do whatever they want to do and be whoever they want to be without being tied down to a 9 to 5 job.

You may find that your WHY is more tied with living a happy, rewarding lifestyle that lets you experience and fulfill your passions.

The money might be your 'what' but deep down the income may only be a means to reaching your real WHY.

Think about it like this: if money was no object, what would you be doing? If you weren't dragging yourself to your 9 to 5 grind to earn an income, what would you spend your time doing instead? What would you buy? Who would you spend time with and where would you spend that time?

Your WHY may be completely different to everyone else's, but it's important you take some time to focus on the type of life you're aiming at creating for yourself.

When you know WHY you want to build a successful network marketing business, you have a much clearer path ahead of you that will make it easier for you to reach your goals.

> *"Time is more value than money. You can get more money, but you cannot get more time."*
>
> *— Jim Rohn*

Chapter Two

Why this business model is for you

Do you know WHY you want to get into a network marketing business model rather than a traditional business?

For most people, the simplicity of having a proven business model to follow is very attractive. However, there are lots of other important aspects regarding the network marketing business model to take into account.

Think about this: when you were in school, what type of skills did you learn? If you're a baby boomer or you're in the Gen Y group, it's likely the skills you learned may be somewhat outdated.

Technology has moved so quickly in recent years that the skills many people learned are no longer valid. This means that the new jobs being created now simply don't apply to people who haven't got the skills needed to fill those roles.
What it also means is that as more companies start to downsize and replace humans with more and more technology, this leaves people searching for something they can do to generate income without having to go to college for 4 years to earn a degree.

This is where network marketing becomes an attractive option for a large cross-section of the population.

The vast majority of direct selling companies take pride in the level of training and support they offer all their distributors. This lets new recruits earn money even while they're still learning the skills needed to succeed. For those people who may have been retrenched or replaced by technology, this is an important opportunity to retrain with an entirely new skill set that can be very profitable.

Even if you do have a job, the amount you can earn each week is often limited. You may be on a fixed salary, or you may only be required to work for a limited number of hours per week. You don't have these same restrictions placed on your income when you own your own home-based network marketing business.

You're able to expand your business to be as large or as small as you want it to be. The amount of money you earn is completely up to you. As technology changes, the network marketing company you work with is very likely to offer more training to make sure you always have the skills you need to stay successful.

You won't be left behind as you be would with a regular job. Furthermore, the network marketing model leverages the time and efforts of your team, no matter what the economy is doing.

So you need to work out what's important to you.

What is your plan for your life over the next 12 months? What does your plan look like in 3 years' time? Will you still be doing exactly what you're doing right now? Or will you be creating income from your own home based business?

Chapter Two: Why this business model is for you

You may not want to work full-time at all, but having the freedom to earn an income around your family commitments might be an important goal for you.

Think about what your own goals and dreams are and then review the pros and cons for network marketing businesses and see if this type of business model might help you achieve those goals.

> *"If you do what you've always done, you'll get what you've always gotten."*
>
> *— Tony Robbins*

Chapter Three

What should you look for in a network marketing company?

Regardless of how awesome any network marketing company may appear on the surface, it's vitally important that you check out a few things before you jump aboard.

Take a step back from the feelings of urgency the sales spiel stirred up in you and think about the company on a logical level for a moment. Remember, you're making a business decision here, so make the effort to remove the emotional factors for just a minute.

One of the first things you want to look at are the products available. After all, promoting those products is how you'll be making some of your income, so it's important that you're dealing with something you can enjoy or believe in or get passionate about.

Think about what sets those products apart from items anyone can buy from a retail store. Is the quality better? Is the brand unique? Is it a powerful item with a growing market demand?

Once you've checked out the products you'll be distributing, it's time to look closely at the company itself. What makes the company stand out for you? What makes it different from other direct selling companies out there?

Some of the larger companies have grown to become publicly listed companies on the New York Stock Exchange, and various other stock exchanges around the world. This means they must disclose financial information publicly, such as the company earnings. Take a look at a couple of years' worth of financial information and see if the company is still growing strongly.

A solid, reputable company will be a proud member of various industry groups. Check that the company you're considering is a member of the Direct Selling Association (DSA - **www.dsa.org**) and the Association of Network Marketing Professionals (ANMP - **www.anmp.com**).

When you've worked out that you're dealing with a reputable company with a strong history and indications of future growth, it's time to look at what the company can offer you.

Take a look at the level of support and training they offer to all new members. The training you receive can be invaluable for helping you get started on the right foot. You should be given plenty of information about the company and the products to help you on your way to success.

Of course, you also want to know that you have access to mentors and leaders within the company if you want to ask questions or find out information. Initially, you might be able to speak with the person who originally recruited you into the company. However, there are times when the person in your immediate up-line may choose not to stay with the business. When this happens, who will take over the role of being your mentor then?

Ideally, you want to become a part of a solid company with a strong interest in helping every single distributor succeed.

> *"The future of network marketing is unlimited. There's no end in sight. It will continue to grow, because better people are getting into it. They are raising the entire standard of MLM to the point where soon, it will be one of the most respected business methods in the world."*
>
> *– Brian Tracy*

Chapter Four

The difference between traditional business and a network marketing business

Did you know that every single direct selling consultant and network marketing distributor is a self-employed business owner? It's true. They're in charge of their own business and as the boss they get to make all the decisions about how their individual business operates.

However, while they're all self-employed they're not in the same category as someone who is working in a traditional self-employment role.

There are some major differences between running a traditional business and operating a network marketing business. In order to compare them properly, let's try to compare the same types of businesses as closely as possible.

Chapter Four: The difference between traditional business and a network marketing business

For the purpose of this example, let's assume we're looking at a traditional business that is selling products from a shop front. We'll be comparing that traditional product business with a network marketing company selling very similar products from a home-based office.

	Traditional Self-Employed Business Owner	Network Marketing Business Owner
You're the boss	✓	✓
Low start-up costs	✗	✓
Paying high rent and overhead each month	✓	✗
Working from home office	✗	✓
Set your own hours	✗	✓
Working strict business hours	✓	✗
Need to buy lots of inventory to fill the store	✓	✗
Paying employee wages	✓	✗
Paying business loan at high interest rates	✓	✗
Paying high advertising costs to attract new customers	✓	✗
Fast Return on investment (ROI)	✗	✓

Chapter Four: The difference between traditional business and a network marketing business

As a retail store franchise owner, back in my 20's, I know all about the high cost of overhead, rent, dealing with employees, cost of inventory, high advertising costs, etc. However at the time, I had no idea that network marketing was a lucrative and rewarding option to income, career and a time freedom lifestyle. Now that I know, I educate others on the remarkable benefits of a network marketing business.

When you look at the comparisons side by side, it's easy to see that someone operating a network marketing business can take advantage of all the good parts of being self-employed. They don't have the stress and overhead costs of running a traditional business, but they have the same ability to generate profits.

So if you've always dreamed of being your own boss but you didn't know where to start, maybe network marketing and direct selling is the ideal business opportunity for you.

> "Network marketing is the big wave of the future. It's taking the place of franchising, which now requires too much capital for the average person."
>
> *– Jim Rohn*

Chapter Five

Understand the power of leverage

In order to really succeed in network marketing, it's vital you understand the valuable concept of leverage.

You see, even though network marketing is a real and viable business, the actual business model used is a little different to traditional business models.

In a regular mom-and-pop store, the customers buy products and the business owners make all the profit, while the staff gets paid a salary. With big businesses, the customers still buy the products, and the business owners may also include shareholders who get all the profits. The staff still gets paid a salary.

Yet with network marketing, the business model incorporates additional ways to generate revenue. Sure, there are still products involved and customers still buy these to generate sales.

However, you also have an avenue available to create residual income with network marketing. Not all your customers will want to buy products from you. Instead, they may like those products so much that they want to become distributors themselves and start recommending those products to their own circle of friends.

At this point, your customer turns into a business owner, but also becomes a member of your own team at the same time. That team member starts selling products and building up a customer base of their own, and a portion of the profits they make flows through to your business.

Now, imagine if you had a team of people recommending and selling products to their customers. Each of those people on your team is building a successful business of their own, but you still get rewarded with a portion of the profits they make.

The ability to leverage people on your team and to help them build their own business even as they're building up yours at the same time, is the true key to success in network marketing.

> *"The richest people in the world build networks; everyone else is trained to look for work!!"*
>
> *– Robert Kiyosaki*

Chapter Six

Evaluate the industry trends

In any industry the trends will change and vary from year to year. In some cases, it's possible to see when a particular niche or industry may be poised for growth, or for a decline.

However, with direct selling and network marketing businesses, the industry trend has shown positive growth consistently over many years. The only exception to that consistent growth was in 2009, immediately following the Global Financial Crisis and the unstable economic climate that resulted from events in late 2008.

So let's take a look at a few interesting industry trends for network marketing/direct selling businesses.

In 2012, the total estimated retail sales made by direct selling businesses in the United States alone added up to more than $31.63 billion US dollars.

That's an increase of 5.9% from 2011, so it's clear that people are still buying products. This also means someone is selling those products and making profits.

However, if you look back to 2000 the estimated total sales made by direct selling businesses was at $25.57 billion. This is a good indication that the industry is still expanding and growing.

Likewise, as job uncertainty becomes more common, the number of people becoming involved in direct selling businesses is also increasing. In 2012 there were estimated to be 15.9 million people involved in a direct selling business. This is an increase of 1.9% from 2011.

Back in the year 2000 there were approximately 11 million people working in network marketing or direct selling businesses. That's an increase of 4.9 million people generating incomes from home, so, more and more people are seeing the benefits of being their own boss.

While these statistics are great for seeing how the industry as a whole is growing, how does it help you make a decision about WHICH company to sign up with?

This is where your research or due diligence is vitally important.

You see, what might have been selling really well a couple of years ago might not be what is trending today. Think about it. Consumers are more informed. They want different things now than they may have wanted a few years back.

A good example of this is the type of products being sold by direct selling businesses.

In 2008, the largest percentage of direct sales was derived from home and family care products, sitting at around 25% of the entire revenue amount. Initially, this might lead you to think that you should look for a company offering these types of products.

However, if you look at the statistics for 2012 you'll see a gradual decline in the revenue generated from home and family care products down to just 21% of the total.

By comparison, the wellness industry was generating approximately 23% of total revenue in the direct selling industry in 2008. By the year 2012 that percentage had increased up to 27% of the total revenue amount, indicating strong growth in wellness products over that period of time.

Likewise, personal care products saw a drop from 22% in 2008 down to just 17% of total revenue by 2012.

Clothing and accessories accounted for just 10% of total direct selling revenue back in 2008, but that percentage has risen to 12% by 2012.

Services and other miscellaneous products show as generating 17% of total direct selling revenue in 2008, and this sector also saw an increase up to 21% of the total revenue generated by 2012.

Based on all these statistics, it's clear that trends do change and what people want to buy will be different from year to year based on lots of different factors. As the population ages, health and well being tend to be at the forefront of many people's minds, so it's natural to assume that the wellness sector may continue to gain in popularity.

Of course, this doesn't mean you should automatically sign up with a company offering wellness products. There are plenty of other sectors experiencing increases, but it's also not impossible to make great money from one of the sectors that may not appear to be so popular today.

As part of your own due diligence and research, take the time to visit the Direct Selling Association (DSA) website (**www.dsa.org**) and check out the statistics for yourself.

> *"Network marketing gives people the opportunity, with very low risk and very low financial commitment, to build their own income, generating asset and acquire great wealth."*
>
> *– Robert Kiyosaki*

Part Two:

Misconceptions of Network Marketing

Chapter Seven

Do people at the top make all the money?

It's common to hear people complain that only the people at the top of network marketing businesses make all the money. They believe that the only way anyone in a network marketing business can make money is to be right at the top of the ladder.

This is a common misconception.

Far too many people hear the horror stories about people getting scammed by pyramid marketing schemes. They're the ones where the people at the top of the pyramid are making a fortune by ripping off people at the lower levels of the organization. Unfortunately, these schemes still exist and people still do get scammed by them.

But network marketing isn't set up this way. The business model does encourage you to enroll new people into your business, but your income isn't completely dependent on it. Not with a good opportunity, anyway.

In reality, the amount of money you make in your network marketing business is completely up to you. You're in control of how you operate your business and you're in control of how big you want it to grow.

You don't have to wait for your boss to give you a pay raise, because you can create additional revenue through your business in whatever way suits you best.

You can choose to spend your time recommending products to customers and making sales, if that's what you enjoy doing. That's going to bring cash flow and profits into your business, so you're in front.

Of course, you can also choose to enroll new members into your team and expand your business further, if that's what you want to do. As your team grows, the profits you make from their efforts grow at the same time. The power of leverage is now working for you.

If your goal is to help others succeed, you can spend your time sponsoring and mentoring each person in your team so that their own businesses become extremely profitable. Obviously, the better their businesses do, the better yours does as well, so everyone still wins. It can also duplicate and multiply your efforts to a 6 and 7 figure income, if that is your goal.

The whole point of network marketing is to build your business and become part of a strong team. As your business grows, you're effectively creating an asset that earns income from your efforts. With some companies, you're able to pass that asset on to children or other beneficiaries if you want. You're even able to sell it to someone else if you're ready for a change.

As you can see, the way you operate your business is up to you. The amount of money you make from your business is also up to you. How you grow your business is also your choice.

You have the option of running your business as a sideline so you only make a few extra dollars when you have the time. You also have the opportunity to really work at building your business up so that it generates serious money. It's still up to you.

The key is to understand that you are running a legitimate business here. If you've done your due diligence before choosing your network marketing opportunity, you should find that the payment model allows you to earn money on a one tier platform and work on selling products, on your own as a side business, or on a multi-tiered platform that lets you enroll new members and thus expand your business and your profits.

Take one of the world's best-known direct selling companies as an example. Surely you've heard of Avon? If you sign up with Avon, you have the ability to earn money by selling Avon products to your customers. If that's all you want to do, that's great! You can deliver the catalogs to more customers or you can stick to your few regular customers. There's no hard selling tactics involved and you don't have to buy thousands of dollars' worth of products just to get anywhere. You can run your business whichever way suits you.

Of course, you do have the option of recruiting other distributors if you want to. Those people can sell Avon products too and you get to build your team, and leverage them.

There are lots of companies out there just like this willing to let you build your business in whichever way suits you best.

It really comes down to checking, researching and verifying that the opportunity you want to join is legitimate. If your research shows you that the amount of money you can earn is NOT up to you, but rather up to where you sit on the ladder – run in the opposite direction as quickly as you can.

Today, companies are meant to provide an income disclosure statement when talking about the money that could be made with this business model. Make sure that the company you choose does this.

Chapter Eight

Do you have to involve family and friends?

Have you ever heard horror stories about network marketing opportunities that encourage you to rope your friends and family into your business? Perhaps you know someone who hounded and harassed everyone they know relentlessly, only to learn that everyone now avoids them.

One of the scariest misconceptions surrounding network marketing is that you need to sell products to your family and friends just to get anywhere in this business. For some people, the very idea of alienating friends and family is horrific. They worry that people will start avoiding them if they keep trying to sell them things. And so they don't approach them at all.

Yet, the main reason so many people DO sign up or sell to family and friends first when they start out is because they're so much easier to approach than a total stranger. You already have a relationship with those people and it's easy to expect that they'll offer you a level of support and encouragement.

Really, you should focus on people who you have influence with, people who respect you and your ideas.

There's also the issue that the people in your family or in your circle of friends may have already had a bad experience with network marketing. The moment you bring up the subject, they may try to stop you or save you or rescue you from being trapped in what they believe, is an evil MLM nightmare.

Now, their experiences might be very real to them. They may also have a strong belief that all network marketing businesses are exactly the same, without ever considering that there are some truly excellent ones out there right alongside the scams.

Always remember that everyone has different perceptions and experiences. If someone has already had a bad experience with network marketing and they feel strongly that you shouldn't be doing it, think about ways to educate them on a different level.

You're never going to convince someone of anything when they already have strong opinions about it. In fact, trying to change their mind or sway their opinion may end up in an argument. There's also the risk that people will stop answering your calls and stop inviting you over if they feel they're being pushed into something they don't want to know about. You really don't want that.

Instead, think about all the due diligence you did before you chose your network marketing opportunity. You would already have access to facts and information about that company and about their products. You would have chosen that business based on the information you gathered and made your decision based on your own choices and your goals.

Chapter Eight: Do you have to involve family and friends?

Here is where I have to jump in and tell you, if it hadn't been for my sister (and best friend) I would most likely not have looked at this type of opportunity. She knew me well enough to know that I was looking for balance in my life and a rewarding career at the same time. This is when I realized a home business could be a very lucrative and viable business.

Rather than trying to persuade people who just aren't interested, why not explain to them that you're starting a new business that you entered into after lots of research. Explain that they never have to buy anything from you or sign up under you if they really don't want to. In other words, let them know that it may or may not be for them.

But also let them know they're always encouraged to ask questions if they want.

The reason for this is very simple. As your business starts to grow and expand, those negative or doubtful friends will be watching you very closely. They'll be waiting to hear the horror stories about how horrible network marketing is or how much you got ripped off, because that's what they already believe. They aren't ready to believe anything else just yet, and that's fine. That's their choice.

What you have is the opportunity to show them with your own actions and the success of your business that they may be mistaken about their negative opinions. When those people realize that you're making profits and you're enjoying your new self-employed lifestyle, they will start asking more questions. They'll start showing an interest in their own time. They'll ask whether the products really work and how much they cost. They'll actually start asking how hard is it to get started in the business.

And all of a sudden you have a new team member who was once totally against the whole idea of network marketing.

Your network marketing business needs to be treated like any other professional business enterprise. You will always find there are people who aren't interested or feel dubious about the idea. You'll also find there are lots of people who absolutely love what you're doing and want to get involved.

If you maintain your integrity and keep operating your business in a professional way, you'll soon find that people become more curious about your success. Work on finding ways to balance your enthusiasm for sharing information about products and a business you believe in with a level of professionalism.

Chapter Nine

Do you need business or sales skills to be successful?

One of the most common reasons so many people put off starting their own business is because they worry that they don't have the requisite business skills or training to succeed.

Now, if you were going to open a shop in a busy mall and hire staff, you'd need a solid understanding of business operations, marketing tactics and bookkeeping just to stay afloat. That's true.

Likewise, if you're getting into a new job that pays on a commission-only basis, you're going to need some solid sales skills to keep getting paid each week.

However, the real beauty of a network marketing business is that you really don't need to study business training or have master sales skills in order to succeed.

You see, the business model makes it easy for almost anyone at all to start a business today and enjoy success very quickly.

The whole point of network marketing is to follow a system that's already proven to work. This means you don't need to have genius-level business skills or years and years of training behind you.

All you need to do is find an opportunity you can believe in with products that excite you. That's more than enough to get you churning profits into your home business.

Yes, you'll find there are things to learn when you're first starting out. That's normal in every enterprise. But the beauty of network marketing is that you have a business model to follow that makes it very easy to move forward and learn as you go.

This is very much like an apprenticeship, where you get all your business training and education at the same time as you're already running your business. You get the advantage of being able to make profits while you expand your education. You're actually earning while you're learning.

You also have a team of leaders and mentors right there beside you, willing to help you every step of the way. They're right there to offer you advice based on their own experience and knowledge, and that's invaluable business training that you just can't get in any classroom.

Of course, if you continue to follow the business plan, you should also find that it's quite easy to start building up your business to whatever level you want to take it.

Chapter Nine: Do you need business or sales skills to be successful?

The whole key to your success in network marketing really isn't dependent on how much studying you've done or whether you have a degree. It's all about how much you're willing to be open to the coaching and mentoring you have available to you and how much you're willing to follow the business model laid out before you.

Most people find that they grasp the structure and system of network marketing very quickly. Once you have a handle on the basics, you're free to take your business in any direction you want to take it.

You can tailor it around your lifestyle and other commitments, which is great if you have kids or a full time job. You can choose to work in your business only during the hours that suit you best.

One of the benefits of this business model is that you will be immersed in business and personal growth training that helps you develop as a leader. Remember though, some companies do not have this option, so make sure to check this out.

And the very best part about it all is that you will find that you also become a mentor to people on your own team.

As you start to introduce people into your team, they'll be looking up to you for advice and knowledge. Even if you're still learning the ropes, you already know more than they do.

There's a really curious thing that goes on when you start explaining things you've learned to other people. Your mind instantly starts to process the information you've been taught in a different way. You gain a whole different level of understanding about any topic when you start explaining it to another person.

This means, when offering advice and knowledge to someone on your team about starting their own business, it actually helps you to solidify the information you've learned from your own mentors.

> *"Screw it, let's just do it!"*
>
> — **Sir Richard Branson**

Chapter Ten

What if you don't like to sell?

One of the biggest misconceptions many people have about network marketing is that it's all about sales. After all, the vast majority of opportunities available still have a product that someone needs to buy at some point.

If you're like most people, you probably hate those pushy salesperson tactics that make you feel uncomfortable. Many people actually end up deciding not to buy anything at all when they feel pressured.

Now, if this sounds like you, it's no wonder you hate the idea of becoming one of those pushy, annoying salespeople that just won't give up or go away.

Fortunately, network marketing really isn't about sales. While there are products being sold, don't think for a moment that you need to be a mastermind salesperson in order to succeed with a network marketing business.

Chapter Ten: What if you don't like to sell?

You see, if you've done your due diligence and actually found a company with products you're happy to recommend to people, you're not actually selling anything.

All you're doing is singing the praises of a product you believe in. When you really do have faith that the product offers quality and value, it's no longer selling.

What you're doing is offering a solution to someone with a problem.

Look at it like this: imagine someone saying to you that they can't find a good widget to help them get something done. Now imagine that your own product range includes a widget that does that exact job.

You could try to sell a product to that person, but that would be selling and you're just not into sales, remember?

Or you could simply say that you use a widget that does all those things for you and it does a great job. What you've done is offered some information about a particular solution that you know already works.

The person you're talking to is very likely to ask for more information. They'll probably ask to see the product in action and their next question is probably going to be "how much does it cost?"

When the buyer asks for information and actually wants to know how much they're spending, you haven't sold a thing. You recommended a solution that actually helps someone get what they want.

Chapter Ten: What if you don't like to sell?

Buyers these days are far more informed than they once were. They research products before they buy anything and they scour the internet for information. While they may have an awareness of exactly what they need, they don't always know the best way to get that item.

This is where the power of recommendation makes such a big difference. You see, they know which widget they want, thanks to internet research. They know there are lots of places out there offering different versions of any particular widget.

What they lack with the impersonal and often anonymous nature of the internet is the personal recommendation from someone they trust. That someone is YOU!

Think about it like this: imagine someone tells you a cool tale about how they found a product that helps them out enormously. They're really pleased with the results they're getting and it makes their life so much easier! As they're telling you this, their voice is really enthusiastic and happy.

That level of enthusiasm really is contagious for everyone.

You see, when you hear information from someone and they're really excited by what they're telling you, it's easy to see that they're passionate about what they're saying. They believe in the product and they're telling you because they believe the product might also be a benefit to you in some way as well. They're not trying to sell you anything. They're simply telling you about something that worked so well for them.

This is the same idea when someone recommends a great movie or a fabulous restaurant. Not only do you listen to them, you do what they say. The great thing about network marketing is now you will get paid for it!

Chapter Ten: What if you don't like to sell?

Now, put the shoe on the other foot. Imagine that's you telling someone about a product you enjoy and you know can offer them a solution. That person will immediately be able to hear your enthusiasm.

That person won't feel as though you're pressuring them into a sale. Rather, they'll be keen to find out more information. That's the point where they start asking you questions and learning as much as they can from you. The next thing you know, they'll be asking when their order can be delivered to them.

So before you believe that you need to sell anything to make any money with network marketing, think of yourself as a person offering solutions. You're really doing nothing more than recommending a great product that could be the potential solution to someone's problem. And that's not sales at all.

> *"Networking is more about 'farming' than it is about 'hunting'. It's about cultivating relationships."*
>
> *– Dr. Ivan Misner*

Chapter Eleven

Can you buy your way to the top?

There are some network marketing opportunities out there that offer people very cost-effective starting options to get them up and running. You might be able to pay $50 or $100 for a starter kit and your business is ready to go.

Yet there are also opportunities out there that deliver slick sales pitches to newbies to the industry that are designed to get you spending more money.

Look for pitches like:

- Invest in the $2,000 kit and you'll move up to the next tier to earn more money

- Buy more product this month and you'll get paid more

- If you don't invest more money you won't move up the tiers

- If you buy extra spots in your own team now, you can sell those at a profit later

These gimmicks and others like them are intended to make you spend more money. There are people out there who are quite willing to pay thousands of dollars buying products in the hopes that they'll advance up to the next level.

The person in your up-line benefits because you're spending more, but what does it really do to **your** business?

Spending money and investing in your business are two different things in this instance.

If you're being pressured to spend more and more money on product, you're not really building your business at all. Instead, you're building a stockpile of products in your house that still need to be sold before you make any profits.

The same is true if you join an opportunity that expects you to maintain a high minimum monthly order just to remain a distributor. If you are expected to order 100 items of product every month but you're only selling 20, your stockpile is getting bigger but your business isn't making a profit.

Likewise, if the only way to earn a higher commission is to move up to the next level, find out if the company offers other ways to earn your way up through those levels rather than buying your way up.

Chapter Eleven: Can you buy your way to the top?

You should also start smelling something distinctly fishy if you're encouraged to buy additional entry level spots in your own team. For example, if your entry level position costs you $1,000, but you're told you can buy 10 spots in your own down-line below you for just $600 each, would you be tempted?

All you need to do is sell those positions to other people at $1,000 each and you're ahead, right?

Wrong. You see, if you spend $6,000 buying those positions within your team and you can't find anyone to buy them from you – you've just lost money.

Then there's the problem of filling the quotas each month for all those positions you just bought. Can you afford to buy enough product every month to keep all those positions active?

These types of opportunities are best avoided. Even better, just run in the other direction.

Every successful business needs to consider healthy cash flow in order to stay alive. If you're spending more money than the business is making, you're going backwards. It's even worse if you pay for those things on a credit card or with a loan, as you also have to worry about paying those off with interest as well.

Healthy cash flow means you need to generate profits before you start spending more money on replacing product stocks. When you sell more products to customers, your business income rises. Naturally, you'll need to buy more products to replace your stock (or get more customers through your online store), so you spend money you've already earned on sales.

As your profits increase, you'll naturally be able to invest more into building up your business. But the key is to make sure you are spending profits and not just spending money to buy your way up the line.

Before you join any network marketing opportunity, always check what your own budget is for your initial investment to get started. Then check if you're required to keep spending money each month (auto-ship) to maintain your distributorship. If those costs are outside your budget, think about other alternatives that are more in line with what you can realistically afford. Some companies offer a program to get your own personal products for free which helps to reduce your monthly requirement.

You can always build up your business after you start making profits.

> *"Don't judge each day by the harvest you reap, but by the seeds you plant."*
>
> *– Robert Louis Stevenson*

Chapter Twelve

Can you really make money in network marketing?

No doubt you've heard the stories of network marketers who have made huge amounts of income from their network marketing businesses. These are the people who show photos of going on luxurious tropical cruises and hanging out at the best beach resorts in the world.

But it's also very likely you've heard horror stories from people who tried and failed miserably with network marketing.

You know the ones. These are the people who jumped feet-first into what they thought was a great opportunity. They hounded and hassled friends and family members until everyone started to avoid them. They pestered strangers to join them in their wonderful opportunity and they spent lots of money trying to buy their way up the ladder.

In the end, those people end up telling tales of woe about how they lost their money and how they got scammed.

Chapter Twelve: Can you really make money in network marketing?

In most cases, the people who failed gave up too early.

Those two examples are at extreme opposite ends of the scale. One set of people ends up doing incredibly well and becoming massively wealthy, while another set ends up going broke.

> *"Don't worry about failures, worry about the chances you miss when you don't even try."*
>
> *– Jack Canfield*

So what's the truth? Can you really make money with network marketing?

In reality, it's very possible for regular everyday people just like you and me to make money in network marketing. The key is to be sure you choose a realistic opportunity with a solid foundation and treat it as a real business.

The primary reason so many people fail with network marketing businesses is due to the 'instant gratification' mindset. They are lured into joining by slick sales pitches that make them think they're going to get rich instantly.

Those types of sales pitches make it seem like they won't have to do any work and they won't have to put in any effort. Of course, the whole idea of money pouring into their account automatically is the real deal-clincher for people with this mindset.

And so they join up, hoping to become overnight millionaires while they watch TV in their pajamas. Unfortunately, this just isn't going to happen.

Chapter Twelve: Can you really make money in network marketing?

In order to make money in network marketing, it's vitally important that you treat it just like any other business, even if it is a part-time commitment while you are still working at your day job.

You really do need to do your homework before you jump in. You do need to ensure that the business model is something that suits you and your needs. You should check that the company is one you're happy to recommend to other people.

You have to understand building your business will take time. It's not a get rich quick type of business. However, even on part-time hours, its common for many to build a six figure income within 1-3 years. Speak with those leaders who have been successful and get their story on how they did it.

Of course, you also have to understand the valuable concept of leverage. You see, even though network marketing is still a real and viable business, the actual business model used is a little different to traditional business models.

Remember, in a regular mom-and-pop store, the customers buy products and the business owners make all the profit, while the staff gets paid a salary. With big businesses, the customers still buy the products, and the business owners may also include shareholders who get all the profits. The staff still gets paid a salary.

Yet with network marketing, the business model incorporates additional ways to generate revenue. Sure, there are still products involved and customers still buy these to generate sales.

However, you also have an avenue available to create residual income with network marketing. Not all your customers will just want to buy products. Instead, they may like those products so much that they want to recommend them to their own circle of friends.

At this point, your customer turns into a business owner, but also becomes a member of your own team. That person starts selling products and a portion of the profits they make flows through to your business.

Now, imagine if you had a team of people recommending and selling products to their customers. Each of those people on your team is building a successful business of their own, but you still get rewarded with a portion of the profits they make.

This type of leverage is the true key to success in network marketing. So can you really make money in network marketing? Absolutely!

> *"You can have everything in life you want, if you will just help other people get what they want."*
>
> *– Zig Ziglar*

Part Three:

The Reality of Network Marketing

Chapter Thirteen

What are the pros and cons?

No doubt you've seen the staggering figures some people earn in network marketing businesses. It's common to see companies showcasing their best performers and highlighting their multi-six figure incomes.

Then there's the other side of the coin. How many people do you hear about who leave the network marketing industry after making no money at all?

The unfortunate part about the massive difference between failure and huge success is that people tend to draw conclusions. They immediately start to think that the people earning those multi-million dollar incomes must be right at the top of the ladder and the hundreds of poor schmucks at the bottom must be the ones who end up leaving the industry broke.

Chapter Thirteen: What are the pros and cons?

Don't be tempted to jump to those conclusions yourself, because it's a complete misconception.

Yes, it's true. There are lots and lots of people right around the world who make awesome incomes from their network marketing businesses. Some make comfortable salaries that let them give up their day jobs. Others make massive fortunes – and these are the people who end up being showcased by companies.

So what happens with the people who give up and make no money? There certainly is a high attrition rate with MLM companies, so what's really going on?

My best guess is that there are lots of people out there who join up for opportunities without really considering what they're getting into. They fall for the hype about getting rich quickly without doing any work. They don't do their due diligence. They start to feel bad about being rejected and so they quit. They may just not have found the right company.

It doesn't matter what the reason is. The whole point is that far too many people sign up with network marketing companies without evaluating all the pros and cons before they start.

So to make sure you don't fall into that category, here are some of the pros and cons you need to consider before you launch your venture.

Pros

Proven Success Record: Did you know that more millionaires are created through MLM businesses than in any other type of business in the world? Anyone who's willing to work at building their business will succeed in this industry.

Chapter Thirteen: What are the pros and cons?

Easy Simple SYSTEM: the real beauty behind network marketing is that it's based on a simple SYSTEM that actually works. Follow the SYSTEM and you should make money. A great way to remember the value of a SYSTEM – Save Your Self, Time, Energy and Money!

Low Cost Start-Up: you really don't have to fork out a huge amount of money to get started in business. You can't start a traditional business for such a low investment.

Tax Benefits: if you're working as a salaried employee you don't have too many tax breaks you can take advantage of. Yet there are plenty of tax breaks available for a self-employed business owner.

Education and Knowledge: you have the opportunity to learn as you earn when you start a network marketing business. You'll be learning valuable business, interpersonal and networking skills, but you're also learning the best way to recommend products, market your business, manage your time and a range of other things that are extremely valuable.

Additional Income: even if you start your network marketing business on a part-time basis, it still has the power to become a profitable additional stream of income for your household. In fact, many people are searching for a Plan B.

Be Your Own Boss: it's a dream for millions of people to be their own boss. You have the opportunity to own your own business with the network marketing distribution model.

Set Your Own Schedule: when you work at home in your own business, you have the freedom to set your own hours and your own schedule. It's up to you how hard you want to work and how much you want to do.

Great Products: if you choose to sign up with a company that has products you already love, you get to enjoy them at discounted prices because you're the distributor!

Expand Your Circle of Friends: one of the biggest issues many stay-at-home moms and dads have is that they can sometimes end up isolating themselves from friends. If you want to increase your circle of friends, network marketing is the ideal way to achieve this. You have people around you in the form of your leader and your mentors, but you can also meet new people and build new relationships with people on your own team.

Support: Team leadership is critical to your success. Make sure you join the right leadership team. As you grow as a leader, you will be helping your team reach their goals and dreams.

Leverage: This business model is ideal for leveraging the time and efforts of others.

> *"I would rather earn 1% of a 100 people's efforts than 100% of my own efforts."*
>
> *– J. Paul Getty*

Cons

Spending More Than You Earn: there are some companies out there that insist that you subscribe to a minimum auto-ship plan in order to remain a distributor. Others will insist you maintain a minimum monthly sales volume. If you can't make enough sales to cover your auto-ship amounts or cover your minimum monthly sales volume, chances are you're paying money out of your pocket to stay in business. This also means you're spending more than your business is making, which could be a ticket to financial hardship.

High Rejection Rates: it's natural for people to say no when you ask them to buy products or sign up with your business. However, the rejection rates can be quite high. This is often enough to deter some people, especially if they take rejection personally, which can lead them to quitting too soon.

Disreputable Companies: if you don't spend enough time researching any company you intend to get involved with, there is a risk of signing up with a disreputable company. Of course, there are plenty of excellent companies to choose from too, but you need to research these in order to sort the good from the bad from the downright ugly.

Low Success Rates: one of the key reasons many people shy away from getting into network marketing is the very high attrition rates. Sure, there are lots of people making huge money in this industry, but the sad fact is that far too many other people quit before they make any money. What most people overlook is that 2 out of 3 small start-up businesses also fail. As network marketing is also a business, it stands to reason that it's not just this business model that could fail – it's actually a normal business statistic.

It Takes Work: while the sales spiel for most network marketing opportunities makes it seem like you can earn money in your pajamas while you sleep, the stark reality is that it takes work to get your business up to that point. If you're not willing to put in the work to get where you want to go, you won't get the results you're expecting. It's as simple as that! This is true for any endeavor you undertake.

This list of pros and cons should give you plenty to think about before you make your decision to get into your own business. As long as you're aware of the potential pitfalls and you've taken the advantages into account, you should be on your way to building a successful business.

Chapter Fourteen

Home business tax benefits

Did you know that operating a direct selling home business gives you access to a range of tax breaks and advantages? It's true!

Even if you decide you only want to run your business part-time around your current job, you can still start to benefit from the tax breaks available.

There are lots of different tax deductions you may be able to claim. These may include:

- **Fuel costs**: if you use your car to deliver products and samples or to attend business meetings, you may be able to deduct the cost of fuel.

- **Car Expenses**: your car is likely to be used more and more for business purposes and less for personal use. The tax office may allow you to deduct expenses, such as insurance, maintenance and repairs.

- **Utility Costs**: if you run your home business out of a spare room, you may be able to deduct a portion of your electricity, gas, phone and internet costs.

- **Home Office Equipment**: your home office equipment may also be tax deductible. Your office desk, your printer, your computer or laptop, and even your office chair may be deductible. In some cases, your accountant may decide to depreciate the value of those items, rather than claiming an outright deduction.

- **Accounting Costs**: yes, even the fees you pay your accountant to work out your tax may be deductible.

- **Samples, Demo Products and Tools**: buying samples to show potential customers or demo products may also be tax deductible. This also applies to any tools you need to purchase in order to display your products effectively.

- **GST**: depending on where you live, you may even be able to claim an input credit on any GST (goods and services tax) you pay on business items.

Chapter Fourteen: Home business tax benefits

It's always important to speak to your CPA or accountant about what you can and can't claim in your home business. Tax laws can vary between states, provinces and countries, so it's a good idea to check the rulings where you live. Besides, your accountant may even be able to suggest a few extra items we haven't included here!

> *"Home based businesses are one of the fastest-growing segments in our economy, and that trend will only continue, as the age of the corporation, which began barely a century ago, now gives way to the age of the entrepreneur."*
>
> *– Paul Zane Pilzer*

Chapter Fifteen

Understand you're not alone

One major problem many small business owners face is that they're in it all on their own. They're responsible for the sales, the marketing, the promotion, the bookkeeping, the ordering and even the coffee making. If you hire salespeople, you suddenly become responsible for their wages and their productivity levels too. It's all on your shoulders.

By comparison, when you start your own network marketing business, you're never in it alone.

This is because the business model is based on building a network. One of the key aspects of success in network marketing is developing a support team around you that helps your business thrive and grow.

Your support team will include your mentors, who will work to encourage and motivate you when you need it. They'll offer advice when you're in a bind and they know exactly what you're going through because they've been there too.

Your support team will also include people you've introduced into your network. Those people will look up to you for advice and support, but you'll be surprised how often some of those people will come up with excellent ideas and ways of doing things that also help you out in return.

The key is that you all support each other.

Of course, there is another major difference between a traditional brick-and-mortar business and a network marketing business.

Let's say you want to start a lawn mowing business. In your new business, you might be able to service maybe 7 customers a day. You are responsible for getting the work done for those clients on time through your working day.

However, you also have a limit on how much you can earn in this type of business. You're limited to the number of customers you're able to charge throughout the day.

Now, let's put that lawn mowing business into a network marketing business model. Suddenly you have 10 people all mowing lawns under your business. They all see 7 customers a day, so now there are 70 homeowners out there with nice looking gardens.

Of course, you also get to still run your own business at the same time, so you still service your original 7 customers as well. Your original business doesn't change at all, but now you've leveraged your business to increase your output by more than 10 times your original number.

Let's take it another step further. Let's assume that all 10 of your lawn mowing franchise owners decide to increase their own businesses a little and they all introduce another 5 new people to mow even more lawns for more customers.

Suddenly, your little home business is being leveraged to create jobs for all those people working under you as well. You get the benefit of that leveraging with increased profits. Those people working with you also benefit by making plenty of money and they also have the opportunity to leverage their own business in exactly the same way.

Everyone wins!

Chapter Sixteen

How much do you have to invest?

Millions of people around the world share the dream of being self-employed. They dream about owning a successful business that lets them enjoy the lifestyle they want and they fantasize about escaping from the rat race of working for a boss in a job they don't enjoy.

Sadly, far too many people never get to realize their dream. They believe that starting a business is way too expensive and they just can't afford it. They think they'll need a huge bank loan to buy into a business that's already running, or they can't figure out how they'll buy an entire store full of inventory just to get started.

What these people completely overlook is that there really is an affordable way to get into a highly profitable business. That business is network marketing.

When you think about the start-up costs, a network marketing business is really quite affordable for most people to get into, as compared to a traditional business model. For example, a franchise can cost anywhere from $250,000 to $1 million dollars.

This is one reason why so many people start network marketing. There are so many different opportunities out there, ranging from very low entry costs, between $25 to $100 for a distributorship that do not include the marketing business kit. These kits will be additional start-up costs and they vary from company to company. It really depends on the opportunity you choose and your financial situation.

The beauty of network marketing is that you're able to grow your own business around your own budget and your own lifestyle.

It's completely up to you if you want to jump in full out with guns blazing and aim at creating a full-time enterprise. Alternatively, you might prefer to start out on a part-time basis around other commitments.

One of the benefits of starting your business part-time is that you have the opportunity to see whether you enjoy working within that type of business model and with that company. You have the opportunity to learn about the business from the ground up and earn some extra money as it grows.

Chapter Sixteen: How much do you have to invest?

Imagine if you had jumped into the deep end and paid for your business with a credit card or a loan, only to find out later that it's not what you wanted. You'll end up with a house full of products to sell and a business that no longer interests you. Keep in mind, nowadays, you do not have to carry much inventory with on-line web stores and the drop-ship to customers option. The internet has improved the way we do business and gives us an easier and better way to build sales volume by the click of a button.

Before you join up with any network marketing venture, always take the time to research the company properly, and understand what the initial financial investment is.

Take a close look at people in the top tiers who are extremely successful and also speak to people who are in the business at various levels within the company. Most of them will be happy to speak to you about their experiences and some of them may even become future mentors, helping you on your way to your own success with their own knowledge. If you're serious about creating wealth through network marketing, I recommend you take in a big event to meet these future mentors in person and get the real deal on the potential of this business.

Talking to people who are aiming at the same goals as your own will teach you a lot about what's really involved in succeeding in that particular business. You'll also have a clearer understanding of what you need to do to reach those same levels in your own business.

Chapter Seventeen

How to avoid high pressure sales tactics

"Today only!"

"This offer is only available if you join in the next 15 minutes!"

"If you don't act right now, you'll miss out!"

When choosing the right network marketing opportunity to get into, it's important to remember that the right time to get into any business is when **you** are ready.

Sure, you might be keen to get started right away. You may have even found some really excellent opportunities that sound exactly like what you're looking for.

But if you're only joining up because that slick, high-pressure sales pitch told you that you'd miss out on earning the big bucks if you didn't join RIGHT NOW, there's something wrong.

There are lots of opportunities out there using high-pressure tactics to get people to join up right now. The key is to recognize them for what they are and make your decision based on your own personal goals, your own budget and your own schedule – not theirs.

Think about it like this: if your success in any company is entirely dependent on WHEN you join, rather than how well you run your business, is that really the type of company you want to join?

After all, if only the people who join up early will make the income, what does that mean for those you're recruiting to join your team? Does it mean they're too late and they are the ones losing money?

More importantly, how can you know that you're really joining early? What if you're one of those people sitting a long way down the line?

What if you join up and only find out afterwards that the company has already been around for years, so you're not really 'getting in early' after all?

The whole point of these slick, gimmicky sales pitches is to get you emotionally involved. When your emotions are stirred the right way, you will feel a sense of urgency. You'll start to feel even a bit of panic that you might be missing out on something terribly important.

But jumping into a business decision on emotion is never a good idea. You need to remove the emotion and make your decisions using logic and common sense.

Always choose a company with a strong reputation for helping all their distributors equally. Make sure to look at the timing in the industry as well, as the market trends of your particular product or service. Is it a company that will be around for years and be sustainable for years to come?

Always look for opportunities that are willing to let you work and grow your business at your own pace around your own schedule and your own budget.

If you feel as though you're being pressured to get involved with something right now, take a step back and look more closely at the reasons why.

Then make your decision without the pressure.

Chapter Eighteen

How much money and time is required?

If you went out and bought a brick-and-mortar business, how many hours a week do you think you'd need to work in order to make a profit? Most store owners would say they work around 50 to 60 hours a week in total, simply because many of them take their work home with them and continue throughout weekends just to make ends meet.

By comparison, many successful network marketers tend to work far fewer hours and achieve far better profits.

Before you get involved with any company at all, make the effort to talk to other distributors about their working hours. Ask them how much time they spend networking and actually sitting at a desk working on their business. Ask them how much time they invest in finding new team members to sign up and how much time is spent recommending various products directly to customers.

Chapter Eighteen: How much money and time is required?

If you follow the systems put in place by most companies, you should find that you're able to generate a decent income in as little as 5 to 15 hours a week for a part-time business.

If your plan is to work at your business on a full-time basis, you still should find you never end up working the traditional 9 to 5 grind at your desk for 40 hours a week. Instead, much of your work may be conducted with friends or new acquaintances over coffee or being introduced to new people at network meetings.

It's completely up to you if you want to invest more time and effort into building up your business. The best part about being your own boss is that it is up to you.

However, it's when the question of how much your business costs you to operate comes up that you need to be a little more serious.

Let's look at an example: let's assume that you're considering an opportunity that requires you to spend $100 per month on an auto-ship option. This means every single month you pay $100 into the company to receive an automated delivery of more products. All of those products get stored in your home until you use them personally, sample them or sell to customers.

P.S. many companies today offer products for free when a certain number of your customers buy monthly, so you can avoid unnecessary monthly costs with this perk.

Now let's say you have a slow month and customers are not buying online or your recruiting efforts are nil. You still have to spend $100 every month, but your business isn't making any profit yet.

Chapter Eighteen: How much money and time is required?

Always look closely at how much you have to spend to stay in business. If you're working with excellent products that people absolutely love, you'll have no trouble selling them quickly. You may even find that your orders start increasing, simply because more customers are ordering even more products from you. In this instance, you're making plenty of profit so the amount you invest into your business is definitely showing some great returns.

The whole key is to work out whether the amount you spend on your business is worth the return you get from it. Then invest accordingly.

> *"You miss 100% of the shots you don't take."*
>
> *– Wayne Gretzky*

Chapter Nineteen

How the compensation plan works

Understanding the differences in network marketing compensation plans can be challenging if you're new to the industry. It's important to know exactly what type of compensation plan is involved with the opportunity you're considering. After all, it is how your business will make money so it pays to understand what's involved and how it can affect your income.

There are several different types of network marketing compensation plans. Before you make a decision about which network marketing business might be right for you, be absolutely sure you understand the compensation plan used and how it works.

You will find some compensation plans that are better suited to those working on building up a part-time business, while other plans will be ideal for full-time efforts instead. Likewise, some will be more geared towards rewarding you for personal consumption or product sales, while others will be more focused on building a strong team. There are also plenty of hybrid compensation plans being used, where combinations of different plans are put together to form something new.

Here's a brief look at some of the more popular compensation plans being used by various network marketing businesses.

Unilevel Compensation Plan

The Unilevel compensation plan is easily one of the more popular compensation plans being used. It's also perhaps one of the simplest forms of compensation structure to understand.

Basically, the sales volumes of any distributors you introduce into your team all count towards your own business's volume requirements. However, most companies using this compensation plan will limit how many levels of distributor will count towards your payments.

For example, if you introduce 1 distributor that person is added to your immediate team. When that distributor starts building a team, those new distributors are added to their team but they're still beneath you as 2nd level distributors for your team sales volume totals. At around level 5 or 6, many companies stop including your original team in the payment structure, so there is a finite depth at which your business gets the benefit for your team's efforts. Some companies will pay out up to 10 levels, while others will cap payment plans at lower levels.

This type of compensation plan is great for those wanting to build up a residual income on a part-time basis, but it's also good for those who prefer to work full-time to build their business.

Stair Step Breakaway Compensation Plan

The Stair Step Breakaway compensation plan is one of the oldest plans around. With this plan, every single distributor you sponsor becomes a member of your front line. As those team members start building their own teams and their sales volumes grow, your business is paid based on your entire team's sales volume.

However, if you have a particularly successful team member in your front line whose volume gets large enough, they'll break away from your business.

Their team's sales volumes will no longer count towards your business's overall volumes, yet you may still receive a residual override income based on their volumes.

While your distributors are building their businesses, your own business benefits from the addition of their overall sales volumes. Yet, if one of your distributors grows large enough and breaks away, you lose that monthly volume but you may not lose the residual income. Depending on the company you're with, you may need to find new ways to maintain your company's volume requirements in order to qualify for residual override commissions.

The Stair Step Breakaway compensation plan does require work, but the rewards can be enormous. You may also find this type of compensation plan is better suited to those aiming at a full-time business.

Forced Matrix Compensation Plan

The Matrix compensation plan isn't overly popular, with an estimated 9% of network marketing opportunities choosing this particular plan. Even though the Matrix seems to offer plenty of advantages over Unilevel or Stair Step Breakaway plans, it's still not used very frequently. There are also some disadvantages to the Matrix, which can mean it won't suit everyone out there.

You'll frequently see plans advertised as paying 3x3 or 4x8 or 3x12 or whatever, when they're trying to explain their payment structure. Some are set up to include multiple matrix levels, such as 2x4x8x16. These are usually set up to pay you commissions up to 5 levels deep.

What this actually means is that the first few people you sponsor as new distributors will be placed directly in your front line team. If you sponsor anyone else after those places are filled, those new distributors are placed into a team below one of your already-sponsored distributors, which is your second level.

Essentially, if you're really good at introducing and sponsoring new distributors, you could start building up the teams of the people in your front line for them. They get the benefit of your efforts as their teams and volumes grow through your effort. However, you also get the benefit of earning additional income as your own team's business volumes grow in the levels beneath you.

Binary Compensation Plan

The Binary compensation plan actively limits your front line to a maximum of 2 people. Those first two people form your left or right leg. Any other people you sponsor are placed into one of those legs below your front line people, so they're still part of your team.

In order to understand how the Binary compensation plan works, you have two sides, or 'legs'. Your distributors on each side start building up sales volume quickly. At the end of each week, your company compares the volumes built up on each side.

The weaker leg is the one with the lower amount of sales volume, and you're likely to get paid based on the amount of volume your weaker leg accumulated.

So if you have $1,000 worth of volume on the weaker side and $1,800 on the stronger side, you're paid on the volume generated by the weaker side only.

What you need to take into consideration here is what the company does with the earnings you don't receive from the stronger leg. Some will carry that volume amount over to the following week. Others will wipe the slate clean and begin a new volume count with each passing week, which means a lot of volume passed through your business that you may not get paid on until you can even-up those legs.

Hybrid Compensation Plan

Some companies choose to create a Hybrid compensation plan that combines the best elements of several different plans. Many of the companies who choose to create hybrid compensation plans tend to put together a mix of the Unilevel and the Binary plans. They're generally designed so you receive spillover payments from your teams as well as override payments based on volumes generated by your teams.

Make sure to understand the pros and cons of each compensation plan before you jump in.

> *"If you're going to be thinking anyways, you might as well think big."*
>
> *– Donald Trump*

Chapter Twenty

How to fast track your network marketing success

One of the biggest things most people want to know about any network marketing business is how they can fast track their way to success. There is no magic button that will suddenly turn your business into an overnight success. There's also no hidden secret that only a few top members know about.

The truth is that there are lots of things you can do to build up your business quickly so that it becomes profitable in a faster time frame. The whole key is to set up your business for success right from the start.

If you set things up correctly, you should find that you don't have to work any longer than about 10 to 15 hours a week. This means you'll need to be focused and goal-oriented in the beginning, but you'll soon find that growing this type of business really isn't too difficult – as long as you put in the initial effort to get it up to this point.

Here is the plan for growing your business up to a 6-figure income in 3 to 5 years working just 10 to 15 hours per week. It's actually easier than most people think.

Step 1: Use Your Own Products

The very first thing you should do is to become your business's own best customer. Actually take the time to sample and use your own products. Work out what you really love about them and what you aren't so thrilled about. In order to recommend those things to other people, you really have to know what those products are capable of doing for you.

Step 2: Stop Selling and Recommend

If you know your products can provide a solution to a situation you hear someone talking about, would you be proud to offer that person some assistance? You're not selling here. You're offering a valid solution that may help that person in some way. The most successful network marketers understand that recommending products to people who can benefit from them is the best way to sell lots of products consistently.

Step 3: Treat It Like a Real Business

Set weekly, monthly and annual goals. Get with your team leader to make sure you are using the start up guide to its full potential, so you can teach others on your team to do the same.

Step 4: Find a Coach to Mentor You

Trying to build up your business to a 6 for 7-figure income on your own is futile. It's also silly, especially when you have a network of people right there willing to support you. Ask for their advice. Pick their brains. Listen to their stories and learn from their past failures. When you have a coach, you have a way to help keep you motivated and help you to stay on track when things don't seem to be moving as quickly as you might want. Your coach will help you with time management skills. This can be a great way to ensure that the effort you put into your business is getting great returns and that you're not wasting time on pointless distractions.

Your coach is also ideal for making sure you're accountable for your actions and your choices while your business is still growing. This can be invaluable for many people who don't know what they should be focusing on next.

> *"If you want to go somewhere, it is best to find someone who has already been there."*
>
> *– Robert Kiyosaki*

Step 5: Invite People to Join Your Team

This is the part many people dread. They fear being a nuisance and they worry about offending people if they invite them to sign up to their business opportunity. So they do nothing at all and just worry about selling their products directly to more customers. There's absolutely nothing wrong with this, if that's how you want to run your business. However, the real key to fast tracking your business is to find people who are keenly interested in making extra money and inviting them to become members of your team. Those team members are the key to growing your business up to the 6-figure income point, so don't be afraid to invite people to join. You'll be surprised how many people are dreaming of owning their own business, just like yours. Some of them will be naturally reluctant, so respect their decision and move on. Others will be absolutely thrilled at the opportunity and could become very profitable team members – but you have to invite them before any of that can happen.

Step 6: Mentor Your Team

Even if you're still learning the ropes of the business and you're still firmly tucked under your mentor's wing, always remember that you already know more than your new recruits do. Use the knowledge you've already learned and pass it onto them. Help them to find their focus and their motivation. Show them how to recommend products for more sales and to get the best results.

Ask them if they're doing things that might be of further assistance to other people in your team as well and encourage them to share. It's important that as your own knowledge grows, you pass on that information to the people in your team as well. After all, as their own businesses start growing, your own business – and your profits - will automatically increase as a result.

Step 7: Create Residual Income

When you work in a traditional job, you're paid for the time you spend working in that job. When you stop working, you also stop getting paid. The same is true with single-tier direct selling. If you stop selling products, you stop making profits.

However, if you're serious about creating a 6-figure income you really need to start focusing on creating a residual income in your business. The ability to create a residual income that keeps rolling in even when you stop working is the true beauty of network marketing.

You see, as you invite new people to join your team, the company should start paying you a percentage of the sales those people generate. Not only are you making profits by selling products to your own customers to start off with, but you can enhance your income by earning a percentage of the sales your team makes too.

This is one of the reasons why it's so important to spend time fostering and mentoring and teaching your team members to build their business. As they start making more sales, your income automatically increases.

Now, if you can encourage your team members to invite people to join their businesses in return, you should find that your company also pays an additional percentage for that additional level. Work with your team and encourage them to teach and mentor their own new recruits, just the same way your mentor did with you and the same way you did with them. This is the ultimate benefit of duplication and why network marketing works.

You want all of those distributors beneath you to succeed in their own business ventures, so offer your own support to them if they want it as well. The more support they have available, the more likely it is that they'll stay focused and reach the level of success they want.

If you can do this, you should find that your income grows very quickly every single month. You'll be earning money based on the efforts from people in your team, which allows you to make a choice whether you want to keep selling products directly or whether you want to focus harder on building up your team's businesses even further.

> *"If you are a person with big dreams and would love to support others in achieving their big dreams, then the network marketing business is definitely a business for you. You can start your business part-time at first and then as your business grows, you can help other people start their part-time business. This is a value worth having – a business and people who help others make their dreams come true."*
>
> *– Robert Kiyosaki*

Call To Action:

If You're Serious About Creating Freedom Through Network Marketing...

Then this is for you! Becoming your own boss and working in a highly profitable home-based business, is about doing it right and taking action.

The information in this book should help you navigate your way through choosing the right company and the right products to work with. You know what you need to avoid being scammed by those less-than-reputable companies out there.

Hopefully, you realize that you really don't have to sell anything to anyone in order to be successful. All you need is a great product and you can recommend it to people who can benefit from it.

What's more, you should also realize that if you really want to set your own hours, work from the comfort of home and achieve financial freedom all at the same time, the opportunities really are out there for you.

Wealth and freedom are yours for the taking, if you make a commitment to working this business distribution model.

Make sure to do your due diligence and research the opportunities available. It does not have to take a ton of time, but it does require your attention. When you find one that really excites you – jump aboard and enjoy the ride. You're going to love it.

> *"You are the master of your destiny. You can influence, direct and control your own environment. You can make your life what you want it to be."*
>
> *- Napoleon Hill*

About the Author

Deborah MacDonald is a successful entrepreneur, speaker, author and real estate investor. Her background includes experience in network marketing, franchising, corporate training, human resource management and real estate investing.

Deborah lives by her purpose, leading and inspiring others to be in charge of their own life, live their dreams and spend time on what matters most.

The vehicles she has chosen to create wealth are network marketing, online marketing and real estate investing businesses. She is passionate about the power of leverage and how it creates residual/royalty type income in both network marketing and real estate investing.

Deborah is a sought after speaker/trainer on sales/marketing, leadership, business development and creating residual income to build wealth. She is also the author of a previous e-book, *7 Secrets to Achieving Your Dream Lifestyle*.

Born in Alberta, Deborah grew up on her parent's farm, travelled the world, and also lived in Italy with her family. She is married with two children, a son and a daughter. Her favorite past-times include golf, travel and personal development.

Bonus Gift

Free eBook - 7 Secrets to Achieving Your Dream Lifestyle

This is what it will cover:

1. **What Drives Us to Success**
2. **The Importance of Setting Goals**
3. **Getting Things Done**
4. **The Importance of Being Mentored**
5. **Systemize**
6. **Outsource Your Life**
7. **Your Ticket to Freedom**

This e-book is designed to help those who are willing to help themselves and have the desire to change. In fact, friends tell me I am crazy to give this book away, that I should be charging for it. The risk associated with free, is you may not do the work.

> **Failure to take action guarantees one thing – Nothing Changes.**

To take the first step towards achieving your dream lifestyle, enter your name and email address at: **www.dreamlifegift.com**.

Made in the USA
Lexington, KY
07 November 2019